Table Of Contents

01

Chapter 1: Introduction to Artificial Intelligence in Ministry

Understanding Artificial Intelligence

Artificial Intelligence (AI) has become an increasingly prevalent topic in various fields, revolutionizing industries and transforming how we live and work. Here we will delve into the fundamental concepts of AI, its applications, and its potential for fivefold ministers such as pastors, evangelists, prophets, apostles and teachers, and Christians who are professionals in the marketplace, business owners, and young people alike. All of them kingdom builders.

To comprehend AI, it is essential to grasp its definition. AI refers to the development of computer systems capable of performing tasks that typically require human intelligence, such as problem-solving, learning, and decision-making. These intelligent systems are designed to analyze vast amounts of data, recognize patterns, and make predictions or recommendations based on that information.

AI has already made significant contributions across numerous industries, including healthcare, finance, and transportation. Every minister can benefit from incorporating AI into their ministries. For instance, AI-powered chatbots can provide immediate and personalized responses to individuals seeking spiritual guidance, offering a virtual support system that is available 24/7. AI algorithms (instruction code) can analyze biblical texts and historical data to provide deeper insights for sermon preparation or Bible study. By embracing AI, ministers can enhance their outreach efforts, engage with their congregations, and strengthen their ministries.

Business owners can leverage AI to streamline operations, optimize decision-making, and improve customer experiences. AI-powered recommendation systems can enhance personalized marketing strategies, while predictive analytics can aid in inventory management and supply chain optimization. Professionals from various fields can use AI to augment their capabilities, automate repetitive tasks, and gain valuable insights from data analysis. Young people can explore AI as a career path, as the demand for AI expertise continues to grow across industries. Educators can also integrate AI technologies into curriculum design, helping students develop critical thinking, problem-solving, and computational skills.

However, as AI advances, it is crucial to consider ethical implications and potential risks. Privacy concerns, bias in algorithms, and the impact of job automation are areas that require careful attention. By understanding the underlying principles of AI, ministers, business owners, professionals, young people, and teachers can actively participate in shaping the future of AI technologies, ensuring their responsible and ethical use.

In short, understanding artificial intelligence is becoming increasingly important in today's rapidly evolving world. AI presents numerous opportunities for kingdom builders. By embracing AI, individuals can enhance their ministries, streamline operations, augment their capabilities, explore new career paths, and transform education. However, it is essential to approach AI with a sense of responsibility and ethical consciousness, addressing potential risks and ensuring that its implementation aligns with our values and principles.

The Role of AI in Ministry

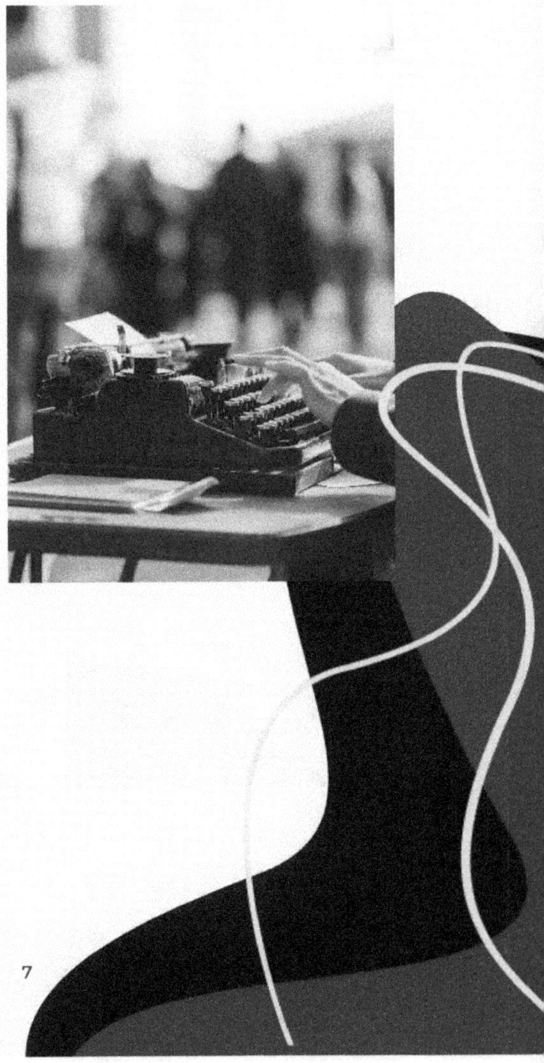

In recent years, the world has witnessed a rapid advancement in technology, particularly in the field of artificial intelligence (AI). AI has revolutionized various industries, and its potential impact on ministry cannot be overlooked.

As kingdom builders, it is important for us to understand the role AI can play in ministry and how we can embrace it in our daily lives.

First and foremost, AI can be a powerful tool for pastors in sermon preparation and biblical research. With AI-powered software and algorithms, pastors can access vast databases of theological resources, historical documents, and commentaries at their fingertips. This allows for more comprehensive and accurate understanding of scripture, enabling pastors to deliver insightful and impactful sermons that resonate with their congregations.

Moreover, AI can enhance the efficiency of administrative tasks within the ministry. From managing church finances to organizing events and coordinating volunteer schedules, AI-powered systems can automate repetitive tasks, freeing up valuable time for pastors and ministry leaders to focus on more meaningful and impactful activities. This not only improves productivity but also enables better stewardship of resources within the ministry.

Another area where AI can make a significant impact is in pastoral care and counseling. AI chatbots and virtual assistants can provide instant support and guidance to individuals seeking spiritual advice, prayer, or counseling. While AI can never replace the human touch and empathy, it can serve as a valuable resource, especially when pastors are not immediately available or when individuals prefer anonymity.

Furthermore, AI can assist in reaching out to the younger generation and engaging them in ministry. Today's youth are digital natives, and AI-powered tools, such as interactive apps, virtual reality experiences, and personalized content, can help pastors connect with them on their terms. By embracing AI, pastors can bridge the generational gap and create innovative ways to spread the message of love, hope, and faith.

However, it is important to approach the integration of AI in ministry with caution and discernment. As with any technology, ethical considerations and potential pitfalls must be taken into account. AI should never replace the essential elements of human connection, community, and genuine relationships within the church. It should be seen as a tool that augments and enhances ministry, rather than replacing the role of pastors and leaders.

AI has the potential to revolutionize ministry in numerous ways. From sermon preparation and administrative tasks to pastoral care and engaging the younger generation, AI can be a valuable resource for kingdom builders. By embracing AI and leveraging its capabilities, we can enhance our ministry efforts and reach more people with the transformative message of God's love and grace.

Benefits of Embracing AI in Ministry

In today's rapidly advancing technological landscape, it is crucial for kingdom builders to understand the benefits of embracing artificial intelligence (AI) in ministry. AI has the potential to revolutionize the way we approach and engage with our faith, creating new opportunities for growth, outreach, and spiritual development. Here, we will explore some of the key benefits that AI can bring to the realm of ministry.

1. Enhanced Communication: AI-powered chatbots and virtual assistants can streamline communication processes within ministries. These intelligent systems can answer frequently asked questions, provide guidance, and offer support to individuals seeking spiritual advice. By automating these tasks, pastors and ministry leaders can free up valuable time to focus on more nuanced and personalized aspects of their work.

2. Personalized Spiritual Guidance: AI algorithms can analyze vast amounts of data, allowing pastors to gain deeper insights into the spiritual needs and preferences of their congregation. By understanding individual preferences, AI can help pastors tailor their sermons, counseling sessions, and other interactions to meet the specific needs of each person. This personalized approach fosters a deeper sense of connection and engagement within the community.

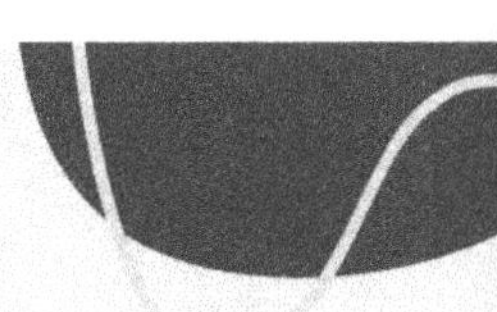

3. Efficient Administrative Processes: Managing the administrative tasks of a ministry can be time-consuming and overwhelming. AI-powered systems can automate administrative processes such as scheduling, event management, and data analysis. This not only saves time but also reduces the likelihood of errors and frees up ministry leaders to focus on more meaningful and impactful work.

4. Data-Driven Decision Making: AI can provide valuable insights into ministry operations, allowing pastors and leaders to make data-driven decisions. By analyzing patterns and trends within their congregation, ministries can identify areas for improvement, tailor their programs to better meet the needs of their community, and allocate resources more effectively.

5. Accessible Education and Resources: AI can democratize access to spiritual education and resources. Virtual classrooms and online platforms powered by AI algorithms can provide affordable and accessible learning opportunities for individuals seeking to deepen their faith. Additionally, AI-powered translation tools can break down language barriers and make spiritual teachings accessible to a global audience.

As kingdom builders, understanding and embracing AI in ministry can unlock a world of possibilities. By harnessing the power of AI, ministries can enhance communication, provide personalized spiritual guidance, streamline administrative processes, make data-driven decisions, and provide accessible education and resources. By embracing AI, we can leverage technology to strengthen our ministry and create a more connected and vibrant community of faith.

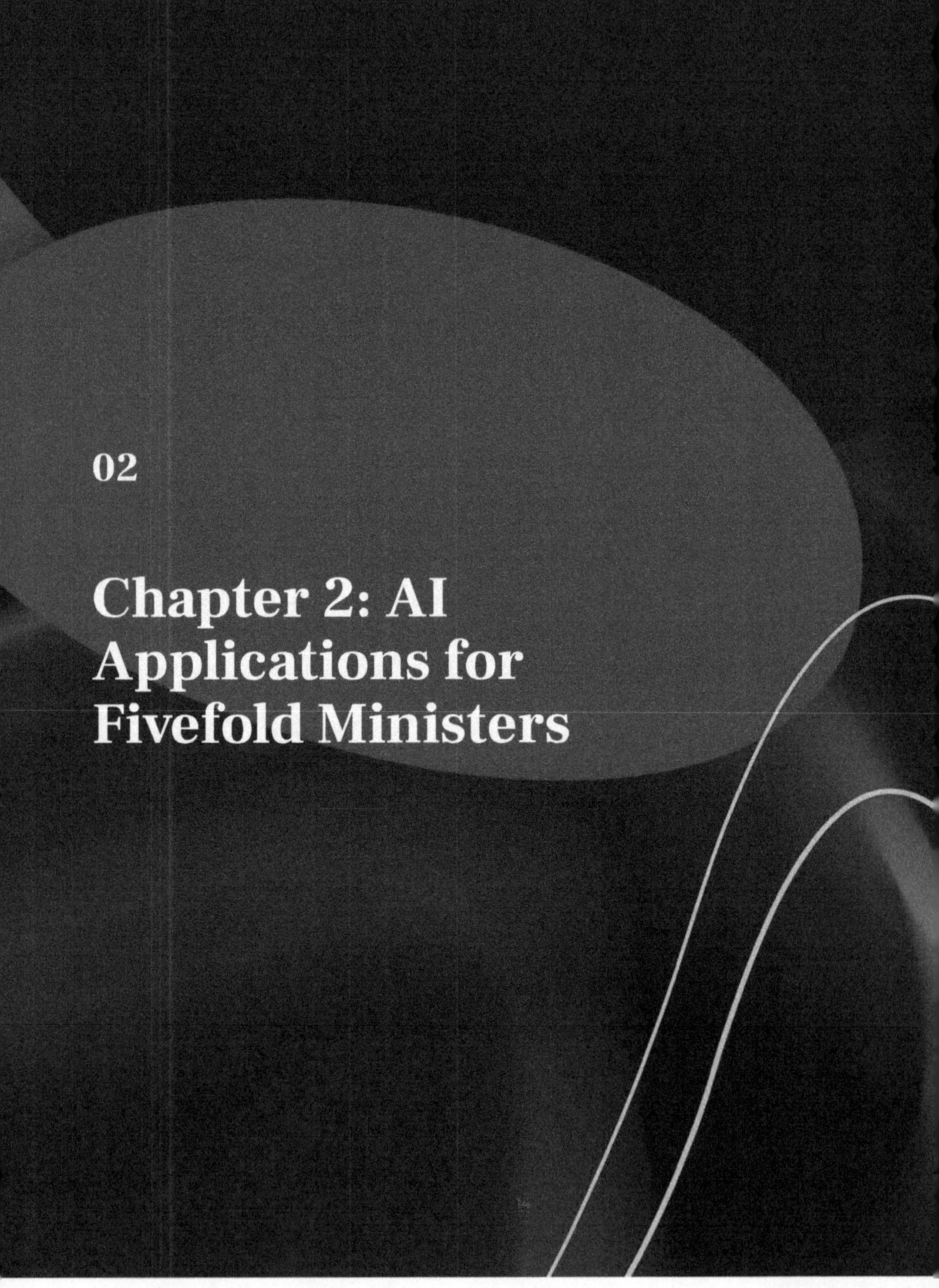

Chapter 2: AI Applications for Fivefold Ministers

Enhancing Sermon Preparation and Delivery

In today's fast-paced world, pastors face the challenge of connecting with their congregation on a deeper level while also keeping up with the demands of their busy schedules. With the advent of artificial intelligence (AI), pastors now have a powerful tool at their disposal to enhance their sermon preparation and delivery.

AI can assist pastors by providing access to vast amounts of information and resources that can enrich their understanding of biblical texts and theological concepts. Through AI-powered research tools, pastors can quickly access commentaries, sermons, and scholarly articles, enabling them to delve deeper into their study and gain fresh insights. These tools can also help pastors identify relevant illustrations, stories, and real-life examples that can effectively communicate their message to their congregation.

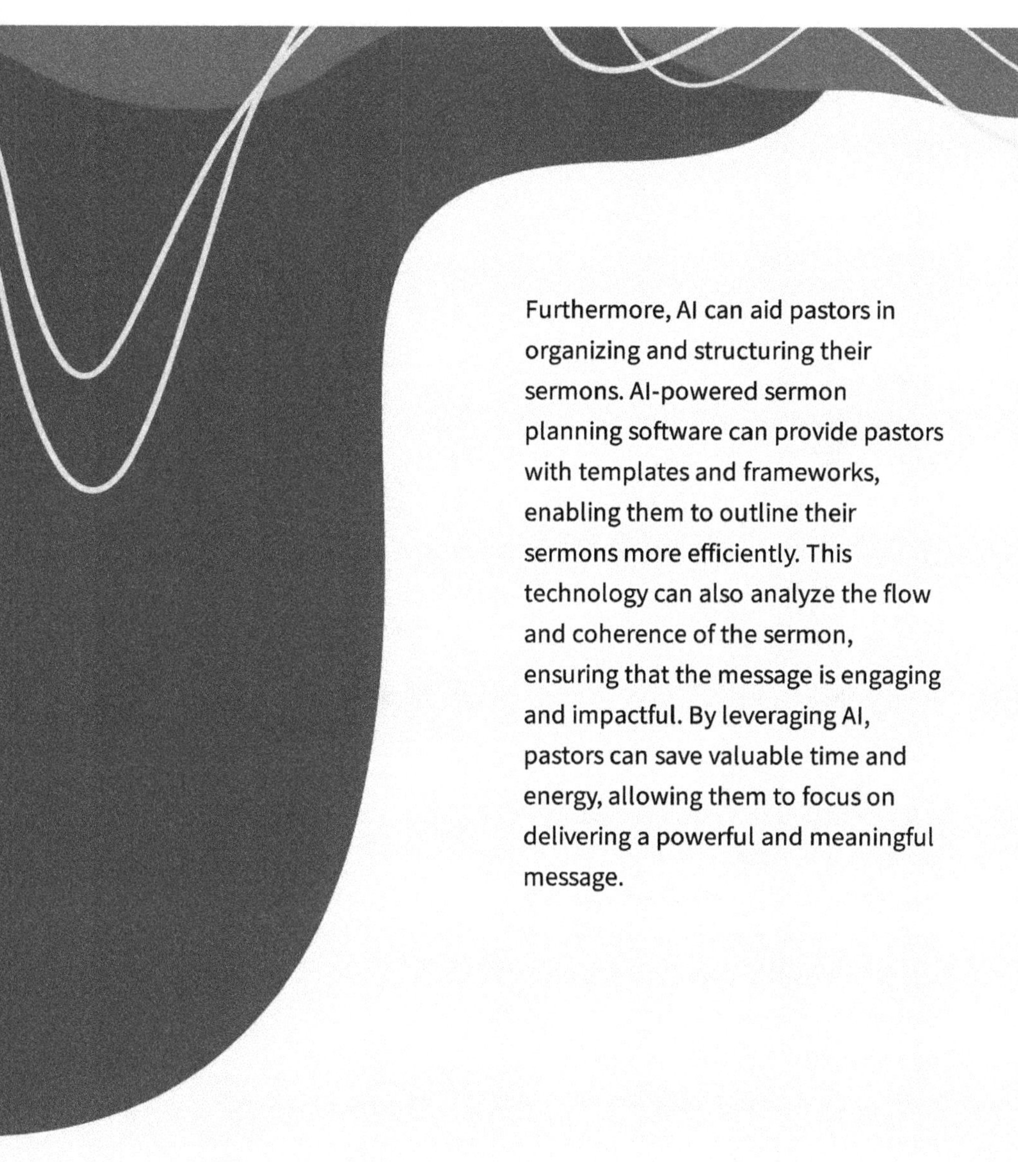

Furthermore, AI can aid pastors in organizing and structuring their sermons. AI-powered sermon planning software can provide pastors with templates and frameworks, enabling them to outline their sermons more efficiently. This technology can also analyze the flow and coherence of the sermon, ensuring that the message is engaging and impactful. By leveraging AI, pastors can save valuable time and energy, allowing them to focus on delivering a powerful and meaningful message.

Another way AI can enhance sermon delivery is through voice recognition and language processing capabilities. These technologies can help pastors improve their pronunciation, diction, and pacing, ensuring that their message is clear and easily understood by the congregation. AI-powered speech analysis tools can also provide pastors with feedback on their delivery style, helping them refine their communication skills and engage their audience more effectively.

Additionally, AI can assist pastors in reaching a wider audience by leveraging social media platforms and online streaming services. AI-powered algorithms can analyze data and user behavior to identify target demographics and tailor sermon content accordingly. By harnessing the power of AI, pastors can expand their reach beyond the physical walls of their church and connect with individuals from all walks of life.

As kingdom builders embrace the potential of AI, they can revolutionize their approach to sermon preparation and delivery. By integrating AI tools into their ministry, pastors can deepen their biblical understanding, enhance their sermon structure, improve their speaking skills, and expand their reach to a wider audience.

Embracing AI in ministry opens up new possibilities for pastors to connect with their congregation and deliver messages that resonate in today's digital age.

Personalized Pastoral Care with AI

In today's technologically advanced world, it is crucial for kingdom builders to embrace the potential of artificial intelligence (AI) in ministry. AI has the power to revolutionize various aspects of our lives, including the way we provide pastoral care to individuals in need. This subchapter titled "Personalized Pastoral Care with AI" delves into the exciting possibilities that AI brings to the realm of ministry.

One of the significant advantages of utilizing AI in pastoral care is the ability to personalize support for individuals. AI algorithms can analyze vast amounts of data, allowing pastors to gain valuable insights into the specific needs and struggles of their congregants. By understanding the unique challenges faced by each person, pastors can offer tailored guidance, counseling, and support, leading to more effective and impactful pastoral care.

AI-powered chatbots are another groundbreaking tool that can enhance personalized pastoral care. These virtual assistants can engage in conversations with individuals, providing them with immediate support and guidance. Chatbots equipped with natural language processing capabilities can understand and respond to complex questions, making them an invaluable resource for those seeking spiritual advice or struggling with personal issues. These AI companions can be available 24/7, ensuring that individuals have access to support whenever they need it.

Moreover, AI can assist pastors in identifying patterns and trends within their congregations. By analyzing data such as attendance records, prayer requests, and sermon feedback, AI algorithms can provide pastors with valuable insights about the spiritual needs and preferences of their community. This knowledge can aid pastors in tailoring their sermons, programs, and outreach efforts to better meet the needs of their congregation.

However, while AI offers numerous benefits, it is essential to remember that it should complement, not replace, the role of pastors and spiritual leaders. AI tools should be viewed as valuable assistants, augmenting the human touch in pastoral care rather than substituting it. The power of empathy, compassion, and personal connection that pastors bring to their ministry is irreplaceable.

Embracing AI in pastoral care has the potential to revolutionize the way pastors provide support to their congregations. Through personalized insights, virtual chatbots, and data analysis, AI can enhance the delivery of pastoral care, ensuring that individuals receive the support they need when they need it. By embracing artificial intelligence, kingdom builders can tap into the vast benefits that AI brings to the field of ministry, ultimately strengthening their communities and fostering spiritual growth.

AI-Based Congregation Engagement

In this rapidly evolving digital age, technology has infiltrated every aspect of our lives, and the realm of religion is no exception. As kingdom builders, we all recognize the importance of engaging our congregations in a meaningful and impactful way. Enter artificial intelligence (AI) – the groundbreaking technology that has the potential to revolutionize the way we connect with our congregations and enhance their spiritual experiences.

AI-based congregation engagement is a concept that harnesses the power of AI to create more personalized and immersive experiences for churchgoers. By leveraging AI tools and techniques, pastors can now tailor their sermons, services, and outreach efforts to meet the unique needs of their congregants. This not only strengthens the bond between the pastor and the congregation but also fosters a sense of belonging and spiritual growth among the worshippers.

One of the key benefits of AI-based congregation engagement is the ability to analyze data and gain valuable insights about the needs and preferences of the congregation. By using AI algorithms, pastors can track attendance patterns, sermon engagement levels, and even sentiment analysis to gauge the emotional impact of their messages. This data-driven approach allows pastors to make informed decisions about sermon topics, styles, and delivery methods, ensuring that the congregation remains engaged and inspired.

Additionally, AI can be utilized to create virtual assistants or chatbots that provide round-the-clock support and guidance to congregants. These intelligent assistants can answer questions, offer spiritual advice, and even provide scripture references based on individual preferences and beliefs. Such personalized interactions not only empower the congregation to explore their faith independently but also foster a sense of community and connectivity within the church.

Furthermore, AI can be utilized to enhance the worship experience through the use of virtual reality (VR) and augmented reality (AR). By creating immersive virtual environments, congregants can feel as though they are physically present in historical biblical events or sacred locations. This innovative use of technology deepens the spiritual connection and fosters a greater understanding of religious teachings.

As kingdom builders, embracing AI-based congregation engagement is not only a way to adapt to the changing times but also an opportunity to strengthen our ministries and impact lives like never before. By leveraging the power of AI, we can create transformative experiences, deepen the spiritual connection, and enhance the overall engagement of our congregations. It is time to embrace the future of ministry and unlock the potential of AI in our pursuit of spreading love, faith, and inspiration.

03

Chapter 3: AI Tools for Business Owners in Ministry

Streamlining Administrative Tasks with AI

AI-Powered Data Analysis for Ministry Growth

In today's fast-paced digital age, the potential of artificial intelligence (AI) is becoming increasingly apparent in various fields, including ministry. As kingdom builders, it is crucial to understand the impact of AI on data analysis and how it can empower ministry growth.

AI-powered data analysis refers to the use of advanced algorithms and machine learning techniques to analyze vast amounts of data quickly and efficiently. This technology enables ministries to gain valuable insights, make data-driven decisions, and optimize their strategies in ways that were previously unimaginable.

One of the key advantages of AI-powered data analysis is its ability to uncover hidden patterns and trends within large datasets. Ministries can leverage this technology to gain a deeper understanding of their congregation's needs, preferences, and behavior. By analyzing data from various sources such as social media, surveys, and online interactions, ministries can identify areas of improvement, tailor their outreach efforts, and provide more personalized support to their community.

Furthermore, AI can help ministries streamline administrative tasks and optimize resource allocation. For example, AI-powered algorithms can analyze attendance records, donation patterns, and volunteer data to identify potential areas of growth or areas that need additional support. This valuable information allows ministries to allocate their resources effectively, ensuring that they are meeting the needs of their congregation and maximizing the impact of their ministry.

Additionally, AI-powered data analysis can enhance ministry communication and outreach efforts. By analyzing communication patterns, sentiment analysis, and feedback, ministries can gain insights into how their messages are being received and perceived by their audience.

This information can help pastors and ministry leaders tailor their sermons, teachings, and outreach strategies to resonate better with their community, leading to increased engagement and growth.

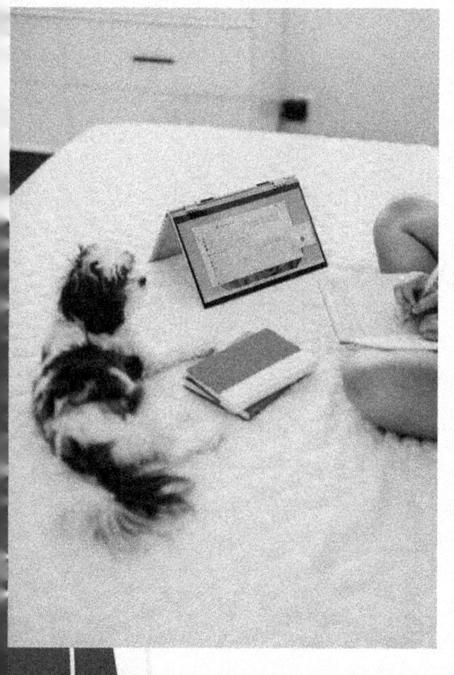

It is important to note that while AI can revolutionize data analysis, it should always be used in conjunction with human wisdom and discernment. As pastors and ministry leaders, it is crucial to strike a balance between utilizing AI-powered data analysis tools and relying on our spiritual discernment to guide our decision-making.

AI-powered data analysis offers incredible potential for ministry growth. By leveraging this technology, kingdom builders can gain valuable insights, streamline administrative tasks, optimize resource allocation, and enhance communication and outreach efforts. Embracing AI in ministry can empower us to make more informed decisions, better serve our community, and ultimately advance the kingdom of God in a rapidly evolving world.

AI-Enabled Financial Management for Churches

In today's technologically advanced world, artificial intelligence (AI) has become an integral part of various industries, revolutionizing the way tasks are performed and managed. The financial management of churches is no exception to this trend. With the emergence of AI-enabled financial management tools, kingdom builders involved in church administration can now benefit from the power of AI to streamline their financial operations.

AI for Pastors: Embracing Artificial Intelligence in Ministry explores the potential of AI in enhancing financial management for churches. This subchapter delves into the specific applications and advantages of AI in church finances, providing valuable insights to the diverse audience interested in artificial intelligence.

AI-powered financial management tools can assist churches in numerous ways. These innovative systems can automate tasks such as budgeting, expense tracking, and financial reporting, freeing up valuable time for pastors and church administrators. By analyzing past financial data, AI algorithms can also generate accurate forecasts, aiding churches in making informed financial decisions.

One of the significant benefits of AI-enabled financial management is the reduction of human error. By automating routine processes, AI minimizes the risk of manual mistakes that can often occur in financial transactions. This ensures that the church's financial records are accurate and reliable.

Furthermore, AI can help churches identify potential areas of cost-saving. By analyzing expenditure patterns and identifying areas of inefficiency, AI algorithms can suggest optimizations, leading to better financial stewardship. This allows churches to allocate resources more effectively, enabling them to fulfill their mission and serve their communities more efficiently.

However, the implementation of AI in financial management requires careful consideration. The subchapter also addresses the ethical concerns associated with AI, ensuring that kingdom builders are aware of the potential challenges and pitfalls. Understanding these ethical considerations is crucial to maintain transparency and trust within the church community.

AI-Enabled Financial Management for Churches provides a comprehensive overview of how AI can revolutionize financial operations within churches. By embracing AI tools, kingdom builders can enhance their financial management practices, optimize resource allocation, and strengthen their church's financial stability. This subchapter equips them with the knowledge needed to leverage AI effectively, making a positive impact on their ministries and communities.

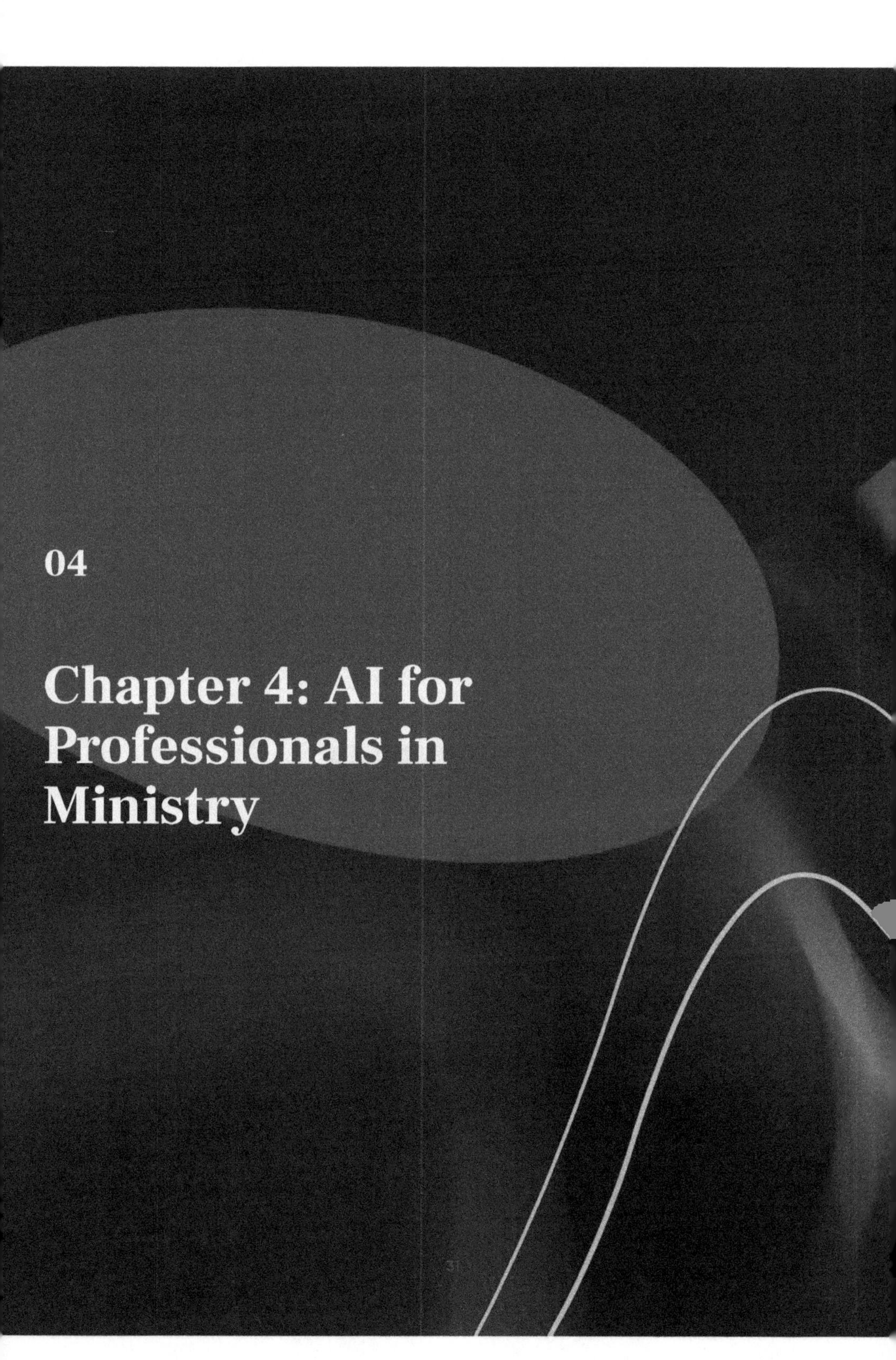

Chapter 4: AI for Professionals in Ministry

AI-Driven Counseling and Therapy

In the realm of artificial intelligence (AI), the possibilities seem endless. From self-driving cars to voice-activated virtual assistants, AI is revolutionizing various industries, and counseling and therapy are no exception. This subchapter explores the potential of AI-driven counseling and therapy and how it can be embraced by kingdom builders.

AI-driven counseling and therapy have the power to transform the mental health landscape, making therapy more accessible and personalized. With the advancements in natural language processing and machine learning, AI algorithms can analyze vast amounts of data, including text, voice, and even facial expressions, to identify patterns and provide valuable insights.

For pastors, AI-driven counseling tools can complement their pastoral care efforts. By incorporating AI into their ministry, pastors can leverage chatbots or virtual assistants to provide immediate support and guidance to individuals in need. These AI-driven tools can offer a listening ear, provide relevant scripture passages, and suggest coping mechanisms, creating a bridge between the spiritual and emotional well-being of their congregants.

Business owners and professionals can benefit from AI-driven counseling and therapy by promoting employee well-being and productivity. AI-powered chatbots can offer anonymous and confidential support to employees, addressing work-related stress, burnout, and mental health concerns. This technology can also provide valuable insights into workforce mental health trends, enabling employers to develop proactive strategies to support their staff effectively.

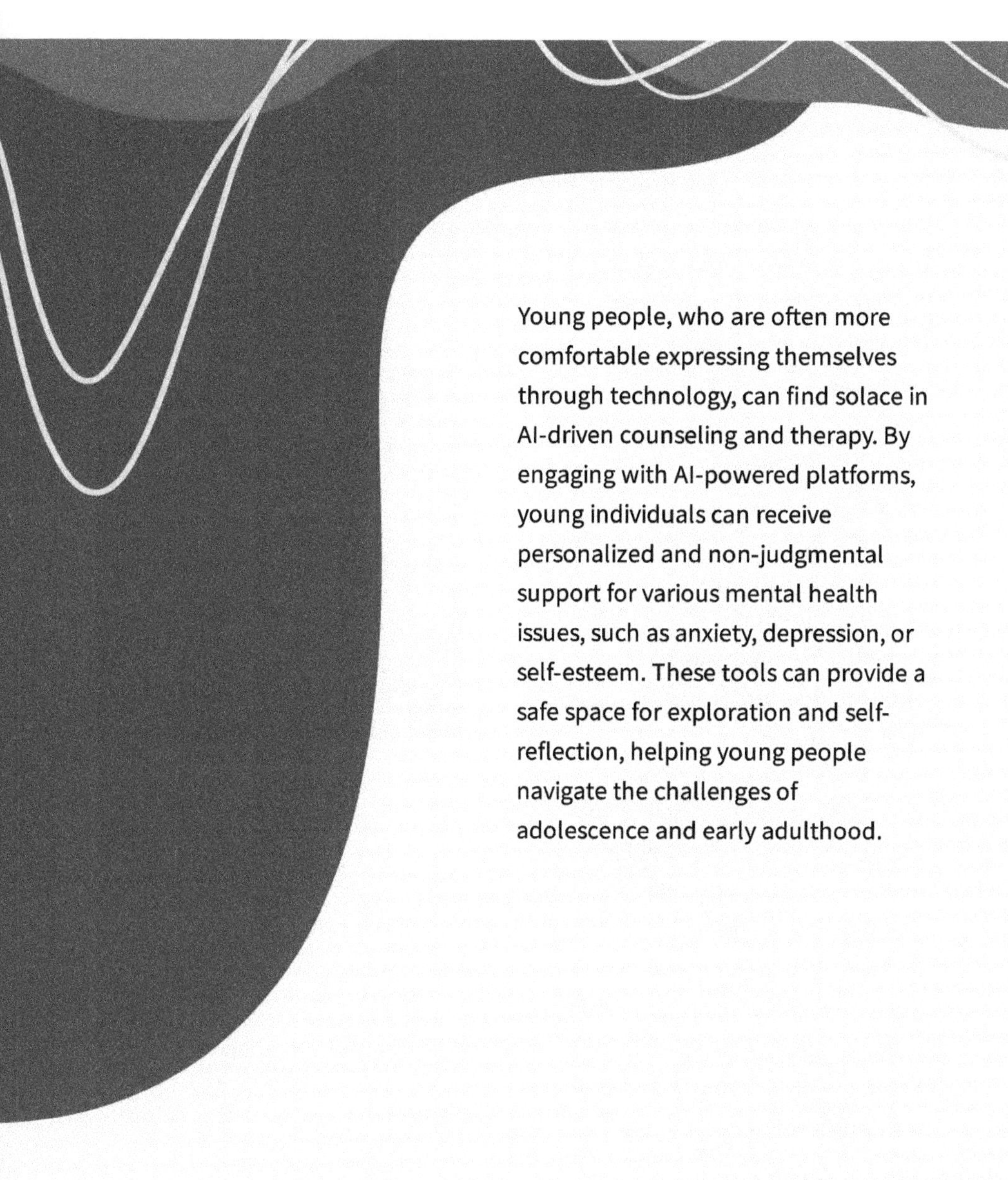

Young people, who are often more comfortable expressing themselves through technology, can find solace in AI-driven counseling and therapy. By engaging with AI-powered platforms, young individuals can receive personalized and non-judgmental support for various mental health issues, such as anxiety, depression, or self-esteem. These tools can provide a safe space for exploration and self-reflection, helping young people navigate the challenges of adolescence and early adulthood.

Teachers, on the other hand, can utilize AI-driven counseling and therapy tools to support their students' mental health and well-being. By integrating AI into educational platforms, teachers can identify students who may be struggling emotionally or academically and provide appropriate interventions. AI algorithms can also analyze student data to predict potential mental health issues, allowing teachers to offer timely support and resources.

Clearly, AI-driven counseling and therapy have the potential to revolutionize the way mental health is addressed by kingdom builders. By embracing AI in ministry and various industries, individuals can benefit from personalized and accessible mental health support, ultimately fostering a more resilient and flourishing society.

AI-Assisted Decision Making in Ministry

In recent years, artificial intelligence (AI) has made significant advancements, revolutionizing various industries. From healthcare to finance, AI has proven its ability to enhance decision-making processes, streamline operations, and transform the way professionals work. However, one area where the potential of AI is often overlooked is in ministry. Here, we will explore the concept of AI-assisted decision making in ministry and how kingdom builders can embrace this technology to enhance their spiritual journey and serve their communities more effectively.

AI-assisted decision making in ministry involves leveraging AI technologies to gain insights, analyze data, and make informed decisions. For pastors, this means having access to a vast amount of biblical knowledge and theological resources, enabling them to deliver more profound and impactful sermons. AI-powered tools can assist in researching and cross-referencing scriptures, providing valuable context and historical perspectives. Additionally, AI can help pastors in crafting personalized messages for individual members of their congregation, addressing their specific needs and concerns.

Similarly, business owners and professionals can benefit from AI-assisted decision making in ministry. By integrating AI into their daily work routines, they can access real-time data, analyze trends, and make data-driven decisions that align with their ministry goals. Whether it is managing church finances, organizing events, or developing outreach programs, AI can provide valuable insights and recommendations for efficient and effective decision making.

Young people and teachers also have a lot to gain from embracing AI in ministry. AI-powered educational tools can enhance the learning experience by tailoring lessons to individual needs and abilities. These tools can provide personalized feedback, identify knowledge gaps, and offer additional resources for further exploration. By incorporating AI into ministry education, young people can deepen their understanding of scripture and develop a stronger spiritual foundation.

It is essential to recognize that AI-assisted decision making in ministry is not about replacing human wisdom or intuition. Rather, it is about leveraging technology to augment and enhance our capabilities as kingdom builders. By embracing AI, we can gain deeper insights, make more informed decisions, and ultimately serve our communities more effectively.

The integration of AI into ministry has the potential to transform the way kingdom builders engage with their spiritual journeys and serve their communities. By embracing AI-assisted decision-making, we can access a wealth of knowledge, make data-driven decisions, and tailor our ministries to individual needs. Let us embrace AI as a tool to enhance our spiritual journeys and deepen our impact in the world.

AI-Based Leadership Development

The rapid advancements in artificial intelligence (AI) have revolutionized various industries, and leadership development is no exception. Here, we will explore the transformative potential of AI-based leadership development and how it can guide kingdom builders to thrive in their respective roles.

Leadership development has long been a critical aspect of personal and professional growth. Traditional approaches often rely on workshops, mentoring, and self-reflection. While these methods are valuable, AI offers a new dimension to this process, augmenting and enhancing our leadership abilities.

AI-based leadership development leverages machine learning algorithms to analyze vast amounts of data and identify patterns. By analyzing successful leaders' behaviors, decision-making processes, and communication styles, AI algorithms can offer valuable insights and actionable recommendations to enhance leadership skills.

For pastors, AI can help in understanding and connecting with their congregations more effectively. By analyzing data related to church attendance, engagement, and feedback, AI algorithms can offer personalized suggestions on sermon topics, engagement strategies, and pastoral care approaches. This can lead to more impactful sermons, stronger relationships, and better support to the community.

Business owners and professionals can benefit from AI-based leadership development by gaining a deeper understanding of their teams and organizations. AI algorithms can monitor employee performance, identify skill gaps, and provide tailored training programs. Additionally, AI can analyze market trends, customer preferences, and competitor strategies to guide leaders in making informed decisions and staying ahead of the curve.

Young people and teachers can also benefit from AI-based leadership development. By analyzing educational data, AI algorithms can identify areas where students may need additional support and offer personalized learning plans. Moreover, AI can assist teachers in streamlining administrative tasks, such as grading and lesson planning, freeing up time for more personalized instruction and mentorship.

It is important to note that while AI-based leadership development brings numerous benefits, it should never replace human intuition, empathy, and ethical decision-making. Instead, it should be seen as a powerful tool that complements and enhances our natural leadership abilities.

AI-based leadership development has the potential to revolutionize how kingdom builders develop their leadership skills. By leveraging the power of AI algorithms, individuals can gain valuable insights, improve decision-making, and foster stronger connections with their communities and teams. Embracing AI in leadership development can lead to more effective and impactful leadership, benefiting both individuals and the broader society.

Chapter 5: Engaging Young People in Ministry through AI

AI-Enhanced Youth Ministry Programs

In recent years, the integration of artificial intelligence (AI) into various sectors has revolutionized the way we live and work. The potential of AI in enhancing youth ministry programs is immense, offering kingdom builders a unique opportunity to engage and empower the younger generation on a whole new level. This subchapter explores the possibilities and benefits of AI in youth ministry, presenting practical applications and strategies for leveraging this technology to create impactful programs.

One of the key areas where AI can significantly enhance youth ministry is in personalized spiritual guidance and mentoring. With AI-powered chatbots, young people can have access to instant support and guidance, even outside of traditional ministry hours. These chatbots can provide scriptural references, answer theological questions, offer counseling, and provide a safe space for young people to express their doubts and concerns. Through machine learning algorithms, these chatbots can adapt and improve their responses over time, ensuring a more tailored and effective experience for each individual.

Furthermore, AI can assist in creating immersive and interactive experiences for young people within the ministry. Virtual reality (VR) and augmented reality (AR) technologies can transport them into biblical stories, historical events, or even simulate different scenarios for them to explore and learn from. These technologies can make the Bible come alive, fostering a deeper understanding and engagement with the scriptures. AI algorithms can also analyze the preferences and interests of young people, curating personalized content, and recommendations to keep them engaged and motivated in their spiritual journey.

Additionally, AI can be utilized in data analysis to gain valuable insights into the needs and preferences of the youth. By analyzing social media trends, online discussions, and survey data, pastors and ministry leaders can gain a better understanding of the challenges and aspirations of young people today.

This data-driven approach enables the development of targeted programs and initiatives that address the specific needs of this generation, promoting relevance and effectiveness.

AI has the potential to transform youth ministry programs, offering kingdom builders a powerful set of tools to engage, empower, and inspire the younger generation. By leveraging AI in personalized guidance, immersive experiences, and data analysis, youth ministries can create impactful programs that resonate with the needs and aspirations of young people today. Embracing AI in youth ministry is not only a smart move but also a compassionate one, ensuring that the next generation is equipped with the spiritual guidance and support they need to thrive in an ever-changing world.

AI-Powered Teaching and Discipleship

In an era where technology is rapidly advancing, it is essential for kingdom builders to explore the potential of Artificial Intelligence (AI) in the realm of teaching and discipleship. This subchapter aims to shed light on how AI can revolutionize the way we approach education and spiritual growth.

AI-powered teaching brings forth a myriad of benefits, enabling personalized learning experiences for individuals. By analyzing vast amounts of data and understanding the unique needs and learning styles of each student, AI algorithms can design tailored lesson plans and learning materials. This technology empowers pastors, teachers, and professionals to deliver content that is specific to the individual's strengths, weaknesses, and interests, fostering greater engagement and retention.

Moreover, AI can enhance discipleship by providing personalized spiritual guidance. By analyzing an individual's behavior patterns, preferences, and spiritual journey, AI algorithms can recommend relevant scripture verses, devotionals, podcasts, and sermons. This level of personalization ensures that individuals receive guidance that resonates with their specific spiritual needs, leading to a deeper and more meaningful relationship with God.

Additionally, AI can facilitate effective communication and interaction within faith communities. Chatbots, powered by AI, can provide instant responses to common questions, freeing up pastors' time to focus on more complex matters. These chatbots can also assist in scheduling appointments, organizing events, and even offering prayer support, ensuring that individuals feel heard and supported in their spiritual journey.

However, it is important to approach AI integration in teaching and discipleship with caution. While AI can greatly enhance efficiency and personalization, it should never replace the human touch. kingdom builders must remember that AI is a tool, not a substitute for genuine human connection and empathy.

 AI-powered teaching and discipleship hold tremendous potential for kingdom builders alike. By harnessing the power of AI, individuals can receive personalized and relevant education and spiritual guidance, leading to transformative growth. However, it is crucial to strike a balance between AI and human interaction, ensuring that technology serves as a tool to enhance, rather than replace, the profound connection between individuals and their faith.

AI-Driven Youth Outreach and Evangelism

In today's fast-paced and technology-driven world, it is crucial for kingdom builders to understand the power of artificial intelligence (AI) and its potential in transforming youth outreach and evangelism. With AI becoming increasingly sophisticated and prevalent, leveraging this technology can help churches and ministries effectively engage with the younger generation.

AI offers unique opportunities to connect with young people who are digital natives and heavily influenced by technology. By incorporating AI into youth outreach strategies, pastors can create personalized and interactive experiences that resonate with today's youth. AI-powered chatbots, for example, can provide instant responses to questions, offer guidance, and deliver relevant content tailored to individual needs and interests. This technology can be integrated into church websites, social media platforms, and even smartphone apps, enabling constant engagement and fostering a sense of community.

Moreover, AI can assist pastors and youth leaders in understanding the specific needs and challenges young people face. By analyzing vast amounts of data from social media, online forums, and other sources, AI algorithms can identify trends, concerns, and preferences among youth. This valuable insight can guide pastors in developing targeted outreach initiatives, relevant sermon topics, and impactful youth programs. By leveraging AI's predictive capabilities, pastors can stay ahead of the curve by anticipating the needs of young people and adapting their ministry accordingly.

Additionally, AI can enhance the effectiveness of evangelism efforts by providing innovative tools for spreading the Gospel. Virtual reality (VR) and augmented reality (AR) technologies, powered by AI algorithms, can create immersive experiences that bring biblical stories to life. These technologies can transport young people to ancient biblical settings, allowing them to witness the miracles and teachings of Jesus firsthand. By merging technology with faith, pastors can captivate the attention of the younger generation, making the Gospel more accessible and relatable.

It is important to note that while AI can be a powerful tool, it should never replace the human touch in ministry. Pastors, business owners, professionals, and teachers must remember that AI is a means to an end rather than an end in itself. It should be used to enhance and support their efforts to connect with young people, rather than replacing authentic relationships and genuine human connections.

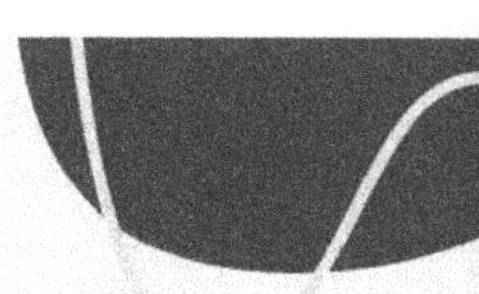

AI-driven youth outreach and evangelism hold tremendous potential for kingdom builders who are passionate about leveraging technology to engage with the younger generation. By embracing artificial intelligence, pastors can create personalized experiences, gain valuable insights, and use innovative tools to spread the Gospel effectively. However, it is vital to remember that AI should always be used as a complement to human interaction, ensuring that the true essence of ministry remains intact.

Chapter 6: AI Tools for Teachers in Ministry

AI-Assisted Lesson Planning and Curriculum Development

In the rapidly evolving digital age, the integration of artificial intelligence (AI) into various fields has become increasingly prevalent. Education is no exception, as AI technology continues to transform traditional teaching methods. kingdom builders alike can benefit from understanding how AI-assisted lesson planning and curriculum development can enhance their educational endeavors.

AI has the potential to revolutionize lesson planning and curriculum development by providing invaluable insights, streamlining processes, and enabling personalized learning experiences. With AI algorithms analyzing vast amounts of data, pastors and teachers can access comprehensive resources and tailor their lessons to meet the specific needs of their congregation or students. This technology allows educators to create customized curricula that address individual learning styles, preferences, and goals.

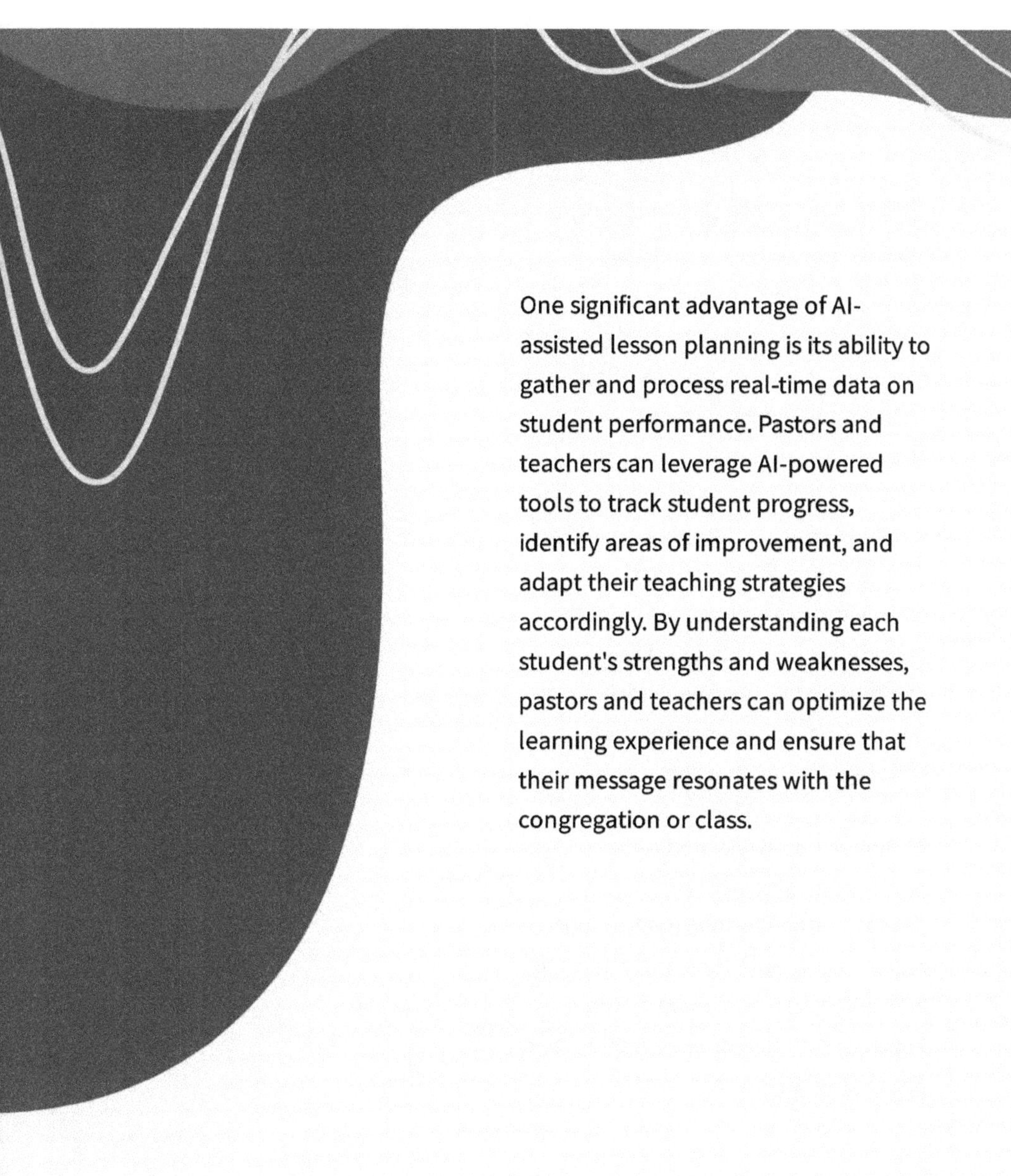

One significant advantage of AI-assisted lesson planning is its ability to gather and process real-time data on student performance. Pastors and teachers can leverage AI-powered tools to track student progress, identify areas of improvement, and adapt their teaching strategies accordingly. By understanding each student's strengths and weaknesses, pastors and teachers can optimize the learning experience and ensure that their message resonates with the congregation or class.

Additionally, AI can provide pastors and teachers with access to an extensive collection of educational resources and materials. AI algorithms can analyze vast databases of content, including sermons, lectures, and educational materials, to suggest relevant resources based on specific topics, themes, or learning objectives. This vast wealth of information empowers pastors and teachers to provide well-rounded and comprehensive lessons, enriching the educational experience for their congregation or students.

Furthermore, AI-assisted lesson planning and curriculum development can save pastors and teachers valuable time and effort. AI algorithms can automate routine tasks such as scheduling, grading, and organizing lesson plans.

This frees up pastors and teachers to focus on more meaningful and impactful aspects of their ministry or teaching, fostering deeper connections and engagement with their congregation or students.

As AI technology continues to advance, kingdom builders should embrace the opportunities it presents. AI-assisted lesson planning and curriculum development can enhance education by providing valuable insights, personalizing learning experiences, and optimizing teaching strategies. By integrating AI into their educational endeavors, pastors and teachers can empower their congregation or students to thrive in an increasingly AI-driven world.

AI-Based Educational Resources for Ministry

In an era of rapid technological advancements, artificial intelligence (AI) has emerged as a powerful tool with immense potential for various industries and sectors, including ministry. AI for Pastors: Embracing Artificial Intelligence in Ministry explores the potential of AI-based educational resources for kingdom builders. This subchapter delves into the exciting possibilities that AI offers in the realm of education, specifically for ministry-related purposes.

AI-based educational resources have the ability to revolutionize the way pastors, teachers, and ministry professionals engage with their audiences and deliver content. These resources utilize machine learning algorithms, natural language processing, and data analytics to provide personalized and interactive educational experiences. Pastors can leverage AI tools to enhance their sermon preparations, Bible study sessions, and counseling sessions.

Imagine having an AI-powered virtual assistant that can analyze vast amounts of biblical texts, commentaries, and historical contexts to provide in-depth insights and relevant sermon illustrations. Furthermore, this virtual assistant can help pastors tailor their messages to the specific needs and interests of their congregations, increasing engagement and impact.

For teachers and ministry professionals, AI-based educational resources offer opportunities to create adaptive learning experiences. These resources can analyze individual learning patterns, identify knowledge gaps, and provide customized content to ensure effective learning outcomes. AI-powered chatbots can also serve as virtual tutors, answering questions and providing guidance to students and young people on their spiritual journeys.

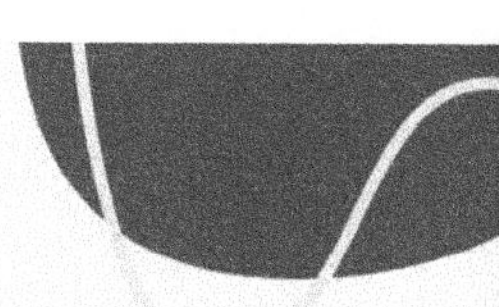

Business owners and professionals within the ministry can benefit from AI-powered resources that streamline administrative tasks, such as managing budgets, organizing events, and tracking attendance. AI algorithms can analyze data patterns to predict attendance rates, optimize event planning, and suggest effective strategies to engage the community.

However, it is important to remember that while AI can enhance ministry practices, the human element remains crucial. AI-based educational resources should be viewed as tools to complement and augment the work of pastors, teachers, and ministry professionals, rather than replace them.

By embracing AI-based educational resources, kingdom builders can unlock new possibilities in ministry. Whether it is preparing sermons, facilitating Bible study sessions, counseling, or administrative tasks, AI has the potential to transform the way ministry is conducted, making it more efficient, personalized, and impactful.

This section explores the potential of AI-based educational resources for ministry. kingdom builders can leverage AI tools to enhance their educational and ministry-related endeavors. By embracing the power of AI, individuals in these niches can revolutionize the way they engage with their audiences, deliver content, and fulfill their ministry goals.

AI-Enhanced Classroom Management Techniques

In today's fast-paced world, artificial intelligence (AI) has become an integral part of various industries, revolutionizing the way tasks are accomplished. The field of education is no exception, as AI is making significant strides in enhancing classroom management techniques. This subchapter explores some of the innovative ways kingdom builders can leverage AI to optimize their classroom environments and create a more engaging and effective learning experience.

One of the key benefits of AI in classroom management is its ability to personalize education. Through intelligent algorithms, AI can analyze students' learning patterns, preferences, and strengths, allowing teachers to tailor their instructional approach accordingly. Pastors and teachers can use AI-powered platforms to design individualized lesson plans and curriculum that meet the unique needs of each student, promoting better academic performance and motivation.

Furthermore, AI can assist pastors and teachers in monitoring students' progress and providing timely feedback. AI-based assessment tools can automatically grade assignments, quizzes, and exams, saving valuable time for educators. Additionally, AI chatbots can provide instant responses to students' queries, freeing up pastors and teachers to focus on more complex and meaningful interactions.

Another AI-enhanced technique is the integration of virtual reality (VR) and augmented reality (AR) into the classroom. Pastors and teachers can utilize VR and AR technologies to create immersive and interactive learning experiences. For example, through VR simulations, students can explore historical events, visit foreign countries, or even conduct virtual science experiments, fostering a deeper understanding and engagement with the subject matter.

AI can also improve classroom management by identifying and addressing potential behavioral issues. By analyzing students' facial expressions and body language, AI-powered systems can detect signs of distress, boredom, or distraction. Pastors and teachers can then intervene promptly, providing necessary support or adjusting the teaching approach to maintain an optimal learning environment.

AI is transforming classroom management techniques, offering kingdom builders a range of possibilities to enhance their educational practices. From personalized learning to automated assessments and immersive experiences, AI has the potential to revolutionize the way we educate and empower the next generation. By embracing AI in ministry, we can create more inclusive, engaging, and effective learning environments that nurture the intellectual and spiritual growth of our students.

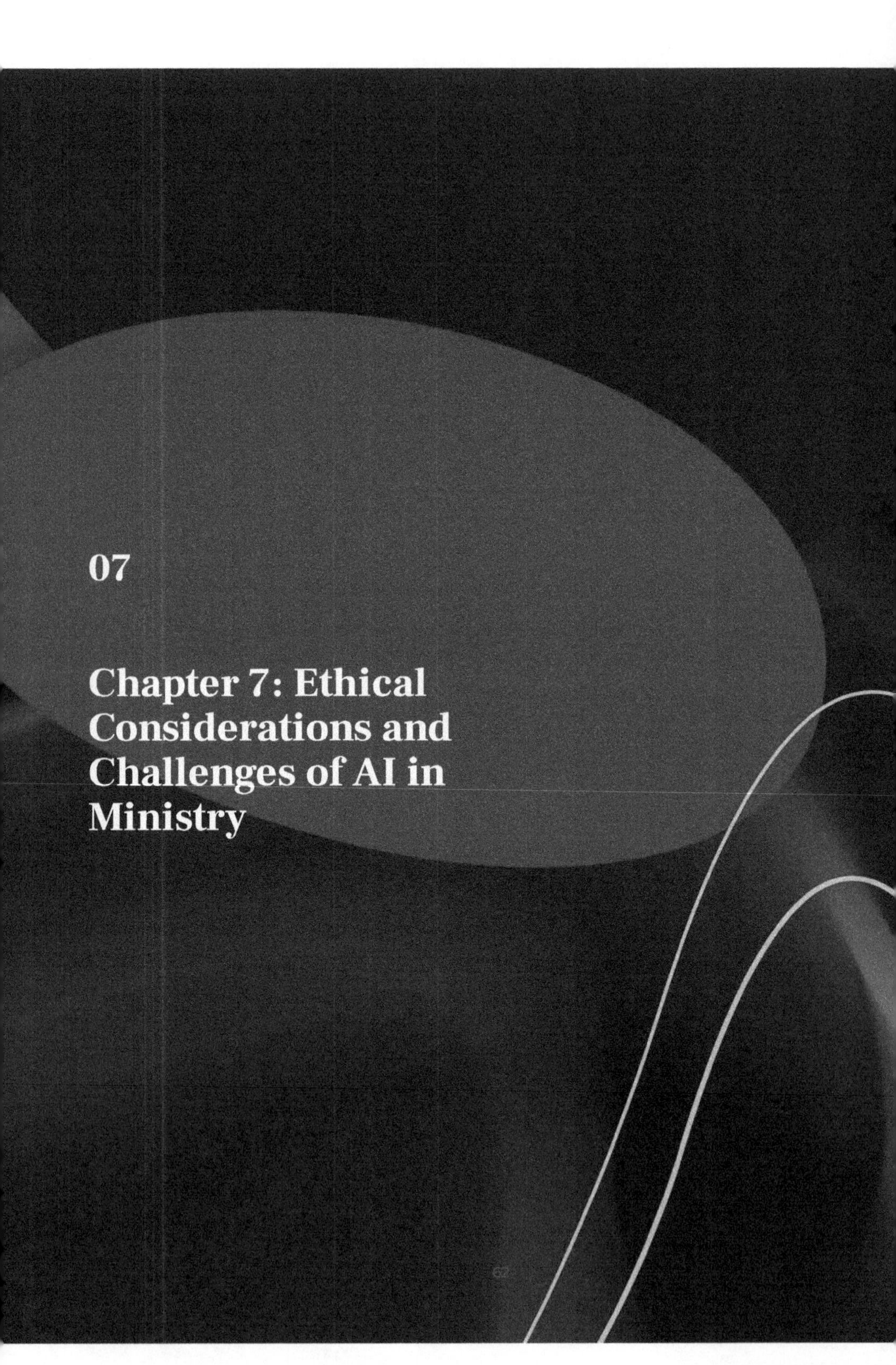

Chapter 7: Ethical Considerations and Challenges of AI in Ministry

Ensuring Data Privacy and Security

In today's digital age, data privacy and security have become critical concerns for everyone, including kingdom builders. As artificial intelligence (AI) continues to evolve and find its way into various aspects of our lives, it is essential to safeguard our sensitive information and maintain privacy. This subchapter explores the significance of ensuring data privacy and security when embracing AI in ministry.

AI technology has the potential to revolutionize the way pastors and ministry leaders work, offering valuable insights, automation, and enhanced decision-making capabilities. However, this increased reliance on AI also raises concerns about the privacy and security of personal and confidential data.

Pastors need to understand the risks associated with AI implementation and take necessary precautions to protect their congregation's information.

First and foremost, pastors and ministry leaders must prioritize data privacy. This means ensuring that all personal and sensitive information collected from individuals is securely stored and only used for its intended purpose. Implementing strong encryption protocols and regularly updating security systems can significantly reduce the risk of unauthorized access to data. Pastors should also educate their staff and volunteers about data privacy best practices and establish clear guidelines for handling and storing confidential information.

Additionally, pastors should be cautious when partnering with third-party AI providers. Before sharing any data with external organizations, thorough research and due diligence must be conducted to ensure their commitment to data privacy and security standards. It is crucial to choose reputable companies that have robust security measures in place and comply with relevant data protection regulations.

Furthermore, regular data audits and risk assessments should be conducted to identify any vulnerabilities or potential breaches. Pastors should collaborate with IT professionals to establish comprehensive data protection policies and procedures. This includes regularly updating software, implementing firewalls, and conducting security awareness training for staff.

Lastly, pastors should familiarize themselves with relevant laws and regulations governing data privacy and security. Understanding the legal framework surrounding AI implementation will help ensure compliance and minimize legal risks.

As pastors and ministry leaders embrace the potential of AI in their work, it is vital to prioritize data privacy and security. By implementing robust security measures, partnering with reputable AI providers, and staying informed about data protection regulations, pastors can confidently leverage AI technology while safeguarding the privacy and confidentiality of their congregation's information.

Addressing Bias and Fairness in AI Applications

In recent years, the rapid advancement of artificial intelligence (AI) has revolutionized numerous industries, including the field of ministry. As kingdom builders, we have a responsibility to understand and navigate the impact of AI on our lives and endeavors. However, it is crucial to recognize that AI is not devoid of biases and fairness concerns. And now, we will explore the significance of addressing bias and fairness in AI applications, particularly within the context of ministry and other professional domains.

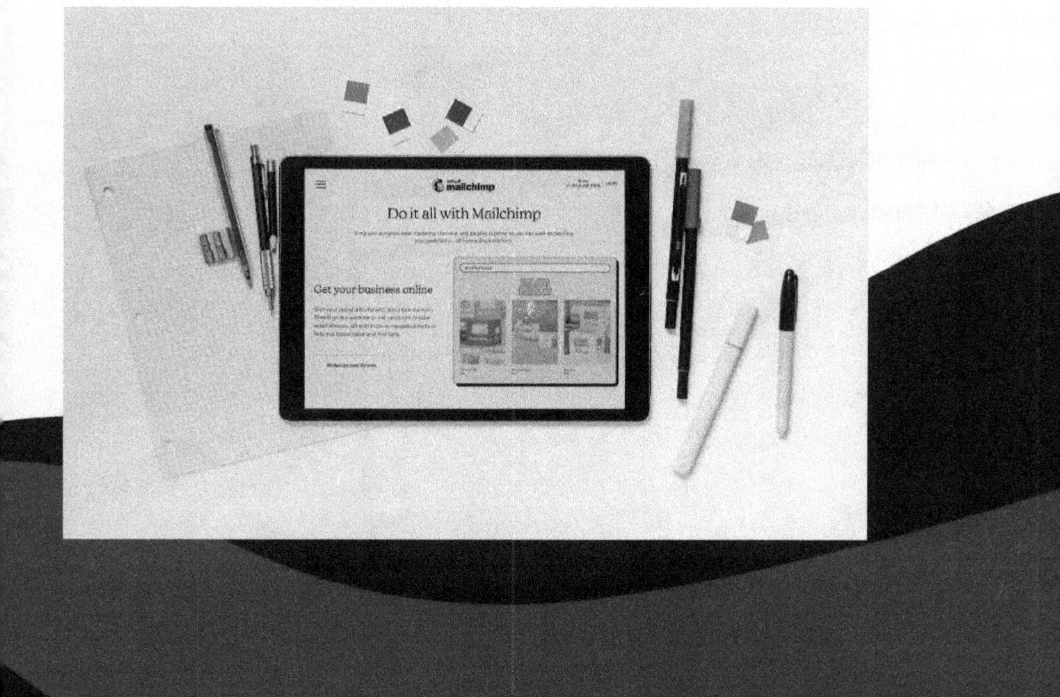

Bias in AI systems stems from the data on which they are trained. Since AI models learn patterns from existing data, any biases present in that data can be perpetuated and amplified in the AI's decision-making processes. This can lead to discriminatory outcomes, reinforcing existing societal inequalities. As individuals committed to justice, equality, and compassion, it is our duty to actively address these biases.

One key step in addressing bias is to ensure diverse and representative data sets. As pastors, we know the value of inclusivity and the importance of hearing diverse voices. By curating data sets that encompass different demographics, backgrounds, and perspectives, we can mitigate biases and foster fairness in AI applications. Collaborating with experts, researchers, and individuals from various communities will help us achieve this goal.

Furthermore, transparency and accountability are paramount. As AI becomes increasingly integrated into our daily lives, it is essential to comprehend the algorithms and decision-making processes behind AI applications. kingdom builders should advocate for explainable AI, enabling us to understand how and why AI arrives at certain conclusions. This transparency empowers us to identify and rectify biases that may be present in AI systems.

Education is another vital aspect of addressing bias and fairness in AI applications. We must equip ourselves with the knowledge and tools necessary to navigate the complexities of AI. By staying informed about emerging research, ethical guidelines, and best practices, we can actively engage in shaping AI systems that align with our values and aspirations.

Now, as we embrace artificial intelligence in ministry and other professional domains, it is imperative to acknowledge and address the biases and fairness concerns prevalent in AI applications. By prioritizing diverse data sets, transparency, accountability, and education, we can ensure that AI serves as a tool for justice, equality, and positive societal transformation. Together, as kingdom builders, let us embrace AI ethically and responsibly, ushering in a future where fairness and inclusivity are central to every AI application.

Balancing Human and AI Interactions in Ministry

In the rapidly advancing technological era, artificial intelligence (AI) has become an integral part of various industries, and the field of ministry is no exception. As pastors and leaders in the church, it is crucial to recognize the potential benefits and challenges that arise from incorporating AI into our ministries. This subchapter aims to explore the delicate balance required to ensure effective human and AI interactions within the context of ministry.

Artificial intelligence undoubtedly brings a plethora of advantages to the table. With AI-powered tools, pastors can streamline administrative tasks, such as data analysis, sermon preparation, and event management, allowing them to focus more on connecting with their congregation and delivering impactful messages. Additionally, AI can assist in providing personalized spiritual guidance, recommending relevant Bible passages, devotionals, or sermons tailored to individuals' specific needs and interests.

However, while AI offers convenience and efficiency, it is crucial to maintain a healthy equilibrium between technology and human interactions. As pastors, we must remember that ministry is about building relationships, fostering human connections, and offering genuine care and support. AI should never replace the value of face-to-face interactions, empathy, and emotional connection that are vital in ministering to people in their times of need.

To strike the right balance, pastors need to discern when and how to leverage AI technology effectively. It is essential to identify areas where AI can enhance ministry without overshadowing the human touch. For example, using AI-powered chatbots for answering frequently asked questions on church websites can provide quick and accurate responses, freeing up time for pastors to engage in more meaningful conversations with congregants.

Another crucial aspect to consider is transparency and ethical use of AI within ministry. It is essential to establish clear guidelines and boundaries for AI implementation to ensure data privacy, avoid biases, and protect the integrity of pastoral care. Pastors should be well-informed about the limitations and potential risks of AI systems to make informed decisions about their use in ministry.

Ultimately, the integration of AI in ministry should be viewed as a tool to enhance the effectiveness of pastoral care, not as a replacement for human connection. By embracing AI responsibly and intentionally, pastors can leverage its benefits while upholding the core values of genuine human interaction, empathy, and spiritual guidance.

This subchapter aims to equip kingdom builders with insights on how to strike the right balance between human and AI interactions within the context of ministry. By doing so, we can harness the power of artificial intelligence to strengthen our ministries while staying true to the essence of compassionate and personal pastoral care.

08

Chapter 8: Embracing AI: Implementation Strategies for Ministry Leaders

Assessing Ministry Needs and Goals

In the rapidly evolving world of technology, artificial intelligence (AI) has become increasingly prevalent in various fields and industries. As kingdom builders, it is essential for us to understand how AI can be effectively integrated into ministry. This subchapter aims to provide a comprehensive guide on assessing ministry needs and goals in the context of artificial intelligence.

Before embarking on incorporating AI into your ministry, it is crucial to first identify your specific needs and goals. Each ministry is unique, and understanding your specific requirements will help tailor AI solutions to address them efficiently. Start by evaluating the challenges and areas where AI can make a significant impact, such as enhancing communication with congregation members, streamlining administrative tasks, or providing personalized spiritual guidance.

Once you have identified your ministry needs, the next step is to set clear goals. These goals should be specific, measurable, achievable, relevant, and time-bound (SMART). For example, a goal could be to increase congregational engagement through AI-powered communication tools by 20% within the next six months.

Setting SMART goals will enable you to track progress and evaluate the effectiveness of AI implementation in your ministry.

After establishing your needs and goals, it is crucial to conduct thorough research to find suitable AI solutions that align with your ministry's values and purpose. There are several AI applications available, ranging from chatbots for automated pastoral care to data analytics tools for informed decision-making. Consider the ethical implications and potential limitations of each AI solution before making a choice.

Furthermore, involving key stakeholders such as fellow kingdom builders in the decision-making process can provide valuable insights and ensure a holistic approach to AI integration. Collaborating with individuals who possess expertise in AI or have experience in implementing it within their respective fields can be beneficial in avoiding potential pitfalls and maximizing the benefits of AI in ministry.

Lastly, it is essential to continually evaluate and review the effectiveness of AI implementation in achieving your ministry goals. Regularly assess the impact of AI on congregational engagement, efficiency, and spiritual growth. Make adjustments as necessary to optimize AI integration and ensure that it remains aligned with your ministry's vision and values.

Assessing ministry needs and goals in the realm of artificial intelligence requires careful consideration and strategic planning. By understanding your specific requirements, setting SMART goals, conducting thorough research, involving key stakeholders, and regularly evaluating the effectiveness of AI implementation, you can embrace AI to enhance your ministry and better serve your congregation in this technologically driven era.

Selecting and Implementing AI Solutions

Artificial Intelligence (AI) has become an integral part of our daily lives, impacting various sectors, and revolutionizing the way we work, communicate, and solve problems. As kingdom builders, it is crucial to understand how AI can be harnessed in our respective fields to enhance productivity, create innovative solutions, and transform the way we serve others.

When it comes to selecting and implementing AI solutions, it is essential to follow a systematic approach that aligns with the specific needs and goals of your ministry, business, profession, or educational institution. Here are some key considerations to keep in mind:

1. Identify the Problem: Begin by identifying the specific challenges or opportunities where AI can bring value. Whether it's automating routine tasks, improving decision-making processes, or personalizing experiences for your audience, pinpointing the problem areas will help you determine the right AI solution.

2. Research and Evaluate: Conduct thorough research to identify available AI technologies, platforms, and tools that can address your identified problems. Evaluate their features, capabilities, and compatibility with your existing systems or infrastructure. Consider the potential risks, costs, and benefits associated with each solution.

3. Engage with Experts: Seek guidance from AI experts, consultants, or professionals who specialize in your field. They can provide valuable insights, assess your specific requirements, and recommend the most suitable AI solutions for your unique needs.

4. Pilot Projects: Before fully implementing AI solutions, consider running pilot projects to test their effectiveness and feasibility. This allows you to gather feedback, make necessary adjustments, and ensure a smooth integration with your existing processes.

5. Data Accuracy and Security: Ensure the accuracy, quality, and integrity of the data used in AI systems. Implement robust data collection and management practices, while also prioritizing data privacy and security to protect sensitive information.

6. Training and Adoption: Once an AI solution is chosen, provide adequate training to your staff, team members, or volunteers to ensure they can effectively operate and leverage the technology. Encourage a culture of continuous learning and adaptability to embrace AI solutions as a valuable tool in your ministry, business, or profession.

Remember, implementing AI solutions is not about replacing human interaction or intuition but rather augmenting our capabilities to serve others more efficiently and effectively.

By carefully selecting and implementing AI solutions, kingdom builders can unlock new possibilities, enhance their impact, and embrace the potential of artificial intelligence in their respective fields.

Training and Equipping Ministry Staff for AI Integration

As artificial intelligence (AI) continues to revolutionize various industries, it is crucial for pastors and ministry leaders to adapt and embrace this technology in their own work. AI has the potential to greatly enhance the efficiency and effectiveness of ministry operations, allowing pastors to focus more on their core responsibilities and better serve their congregations. However, in order to fully leverage the power of AI, ministry staff must be properly trained and equipped.

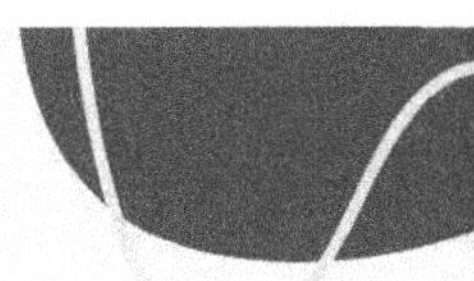

The first step in training ministry staff for AI integration is to develop a comprehensive understanding of the technology and its potential applications within the ministry context. This involves educating staff members on the various AI tools and platforms available, as well as the specific ways in which they can be utilized to enhance ministry operations. kingdom builders alike can benefit from gaining knowledge about AI and its implications for ministry.

Once a foundational understanding of AI is established, it is important to identify specific areas within the ministry where AI can be implemented. This could include using AI-powered chatbots for responding to inquiries, utilizing data analytics to gain insights into congregation needs, or employing AI algorithms to optimize sermon delivery based on audience preferences. By identifying these areas, ministry staff can then receive targeted training to develop the necessary skills for effectively integrating AI into their work.

Training should not be limited to technical skills alone. It is equally important to equip ministry staff with the mindset and values needed to navigate the ethical considerations surrounding AI. This includes discussing topics such as data privacy, bias in algorithms, and the potential impact of AI on human relationships. By fostering a culture of ethical AI use, pastors and ministry staff can ensure that this technology aligns with their core values and enhances their mission rather than detracting from it.

Furthermore, ongoing professional development and continuous learning opportunities should be provided to ministry staff to keep them updated on the latest AI advancements. This could include attending conferences, participating in webinars, or engaging with AI experts in the field. By investing in the growth and development of staff members, pastors can create a dynamic and forward-thinking ministry that remains at the forefront of AI integration.

So, training and equipping ministry staff for AI integration is crucial for pastors and ministry leaders looking to embrace the potential of this technology. By providing comprehensive education, targeted training, and ongoing professional development, pastors can ensure that ministry staff are well-prepared to leverage AI tools and platforms to enhance their work. This will ultimately lead to more efficient operations, improved service to congregations, and a ministry that remains relevant in an increasingly AI-driven world.

09

Chapter 9: The Future of AI in Ministry

Emerging Trends in AI for Ministry

As artificial intelligence (AI) continues to revolutionize various industries, it is crucial for kingdom builders to be aware of the emerging trends in AI for ministry. AI has the potential to greatly enhance the effectiveness and efficiency of various aspects of ministry, allowing for better engagement with congregations, more informed decision-making, and a deeper understanding of scripture. Next, we explore some of the key trends that are shaping the use of AI in ministry.

One of the most significant trends is the use of AI-powered chatbots and virtual assistants in ministry. These intelligent programs can engage with congregants, answer frequently asked questions, provide spiritual guidance, and even offer prayer support. Chatbots can be integrated into websites, social media platforms, and mobile applications, ensuring 24/7 availability and support for individuals seeking guidance or connection with the ministry.

Another emerging trend is the use of AI for data analytics and predictive modeling. By analyzing vast amounts of data, AI algorithms can identify patterns and trends, providing valuable insights into the needs and preferences of the congregation. Pastors and ministry leaders can use this information to tailor their messages, outreach programs, and community initiatives to better serve their congregations.

AI-powered language processing and sentiment analysis are also gaining prominence in ministry. These technologies can analyze written or spoken language to determine the emotional tone, sentiment, and context of the communication. Pastors can use such tools to gauge the response of their sermons, identify areas where additional support may be needed, and ensure effective communication with their congregations.

Furthermore, AI is revolutionizing the accessibility of scripture through automated translation and interpretation tools. These applications can provide real-time translations of sermons, Bible verses, and devotional content in multiple languages, enabling pastors to reach a broader audience and break language barriers.

Lastly, AI-powered recommendation systems are being employed in ministry to suggest relevant content, sermons, and resources to individuals based on their preferences and interests. These personalized recommendations can help individuals deepen their spiritual journey and engage more meaningfully with the ministry.

Clearly, AI holds immense potential for enhancing ministry in various ways. From chatbots and virtual assistants to data analytics and personalized recommendations, kingdom builders can embrace these emerging trends to better serve their congregations, create meaningful connections, and foster spiritual growth. By embracing AI in ministry, we can leverage technology for the greater good and ensure that the message of love and faith reaches a wider audience in a more impactful manner.

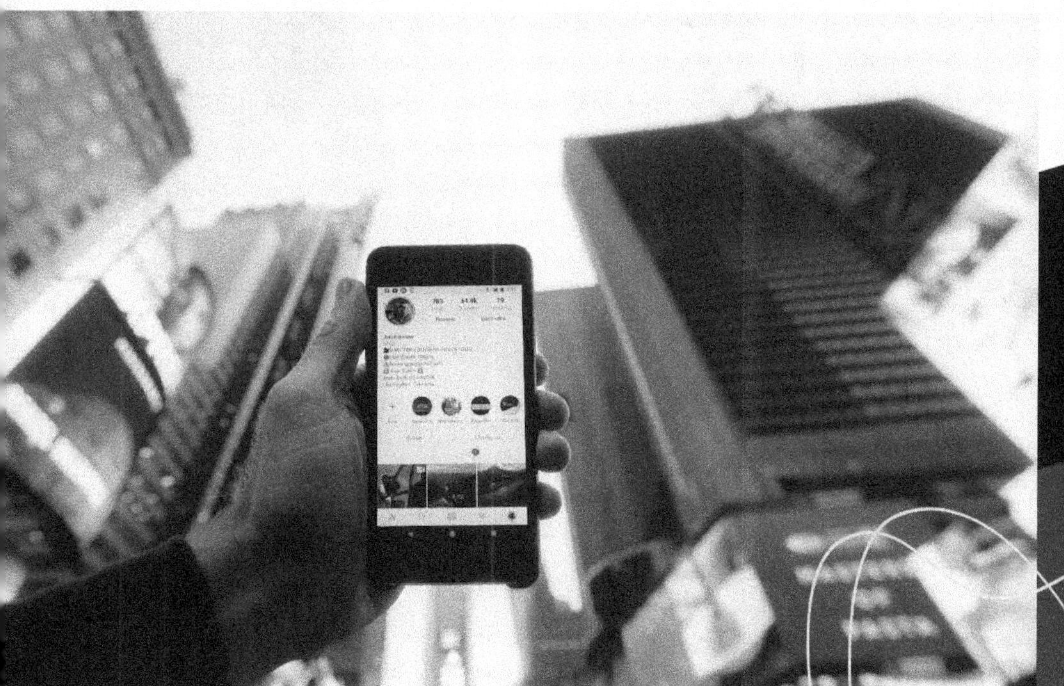

AI's Potential Impact on the Church and Society

In recent years, Artificial Intelligence (AI) has emerged as a transformative technology, reshaping industries and societies across the globe. While its impact is undeniable, one aspect that demands significant attention is its potential influence on the Church and society as a whole. Also, we explore the myriad ways in which AI can shape the future of the Church and society, and the opportunities and challenges it presents.

AI has the power to revolutionize the way pastors and church leaders carry out their ministries. With advanced data analytics, AI can assist pastors in understanding the needs and preferences of their congregations better. By analyzing the vast amounts of data available, AI can help pastors tailor their sermons, worship experiences, and pastoral care to better meet the spiritual needs of their congregants. Additionally, AI-powered chatbots can provide instant pastoral counseling and guidance, ensuring that support is accessible to anyone at any time.

The integration of AI can also have a profound impact on society at large. AI-powered systems can help address societal challenges such as poverty, inequality, and education. From predicting and preventing crime to optimizing resource allocation, AI can aid in creating more equitable and just communities. Moreover, AI can revolutionize education by personalizing learning experiences, enabling students to receive tailored instruction based on their individual strengths and weaknesses.

However, as kingdom builders, it is crucial to grapple with the ethical implications of AI. The potential for bias and discrimination within AI systems demands careful consideration. As AI algorithms learn from existing data, they may perpetuate existing societal prejudices, amplifying inequalities rather than mitigating them. Therefore, it is essential for pastors and society as a whole to actively engage in shaping AI technologies to ensure fairness, transparency, and inclusivity.

It is also important to address concerns related to the displacement of human labor. As AI automates certain tasks, there is a possibility of job losses, particularly in industries that rely heavily on manual labor. Pastors and business owners must consider the ethical responsibility of ensuring the well-being and livelihoods of individuals affected by AI-driven automation.

Clearly, AI holds immense potential to transform the Church and society in profound ways. By leveraging AI technologies, pastors can better serve their congregations, and society can address complex challenges more effectively. However, it is imperative to approach AI with a critical lens, actively engaging in ethical discussions and ensuring that AI systems promote fairness and inclusivity. As kingdom builders, embracing AI while also advocating for its responsible and ethical use will be paramount in harnessing its full potential for the betterment of the Church and society.

Embracing a Future of AI-Driven Ministry

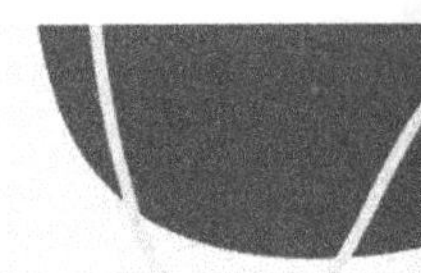

In recent years, artificial intelligence (AI) has rapidly transformed various industries, and now it is making its way into the realm of ministry. As kingdom builders, it is crucial for us to understand the potential of AI in enhancing our ministries and reaching out to people in more effective ways.

AI offers a range of exciting possibilities for ministry, enabling us to streamline administrative tasks, enhance communication, and deepen our understanding of scripture. By embracing AI, we can free up valuable time and resources to focus on what truly matters – serving and ministering to our communities.

One of the primary benefits of AI in ministry is the ability to automate routine tasks. Imagine having an AI-powered assistant that can handle scheduling, data entry, and other administrative duties, allowing you to devote more time to studying scripture, counseling, and connecting with your congregation. AI can also assist in managing church finances, generating reports, and even providing personalized recommendations for sermon topics based on community needs.

Furthermore, AI can revolutionize communication within a ministry. Chatbots, for example, can provide immediate responses to frequently asked questions, offer guidance on prayer requests, or even engage in interactive Bible studies. This technology allows us to be available to our congregations 24/7, providing support and guidance whenever it is needed.

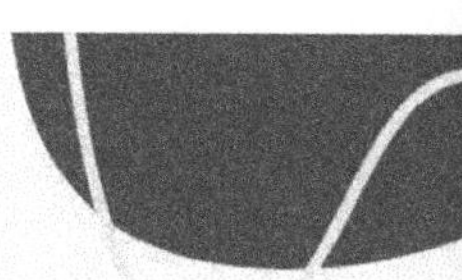

AI can also enhance our understanding of scripture by analyzing vast amounts of data and providing insights that may have previously gone unnoticed. By leveraging AI tools, we can discover new perspectives, uncover hidden patterns, and gain deeper theological insights. This knowledge can then be shared with our communities, enriching their understanding and fostering further spiritual growth.

While AI brings immense possibilities, it is essential to approach its implementation with wisdom and discernment. As pastors and leaders, we must remember that AI should never replace human connection and empathy but rather enhance our ability to serve and minister effectively.

It is clear that embracing a future of AI-driven ministry holds immense potential for kingdom builders alike. By leveraging the power of AI, we can streamline administrative tasks, enhance communication, and deepen our understanding of scripture. Let us embrace this technological advancement with open minds and hearts, using it as a tool to further our ministries and connect with our communities in more profound and meaningful ways.

10

Chapter 10: Conclusion

Recap of AI's Role in Ministry

As we delve into the exciting world of AI for ministry, it is crucial to recap artificial intelligence's significant role in our spiritual journey. AI has revolutionized various industries, and the ministry is no exception. We concisely summarize AI's impact on ministry and its potential implications for kingdom builders.

Artificial intelligence has the power to enhance ministry practices in numerous ways. One of the most notable areas is data analysis. With AI algorithms, pastors can gain valuable insights from vast amounts of data collected from their congregations. This information can shed light on members' needs, preferences, and engagement levels, enabling pastors to tailor their sermons, programs, and outreach initiatives accordingly.

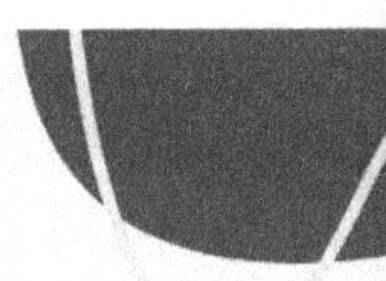

Moreover, AI-powered chatbots have become increasingly popular in ministry settings. These virtual assistants can provide real-time support and guidance to individuals seeking spiritual advice, prayer, or information about church activities. Chatbots are available 24/7 and can interact with multiple users simultaneously, offering a seamless and personalized experience for those seeking spiritual guidance.

Another significant role of AI in ministry is in the realm of content creation. AI algorithms can analyze sermons, books, and other religious texts to identify patterns, themes, and insights. This knowledge can assist pastors and teachers in crafting impactful messages and lessons that resonate with their congregations. AI can also generate sermon outlines or suggest relevant Bible verses, saving time and providing inspiration.

For business owners and professionals within the ministry, AI offers immense potential to streamline administrative tasks. AI-powered systems can automate routine processes such as managing finances, scheduling events, and organizing volunteers. This automation allows individuals to focus more on their spiritual duties and enables efficient resource allocation within the ministry.

Young people, who are often deeply entrenched in the digital world, can benefit greatly from AI applications in ministry. AI-powered learning platforms can provide interactive and engaging tools to help young individuals explore their faith, ask questions, and deepen their understanding of religious teachings. This innovative approach can foster a sense of belonging and encourage active participation within the church community.

Lastly, educators and teachers within the ministry can leverage AI to enhance their teaching methodology. AI-powered educational tools can adapt to students' individual learning styles, offering personalized content and assessments. This tailored approach can help educators facilitate meaningful and impactful lessons, allowing students to grow spiritually and intellectually.

It is evident, AI's role in ministry is multifaceted and transformative. From data analysis to chatbots, content creation to administrative tasks, AI offers a wealth of opportunities for kingdom builders within the ministry. Embracing artificial intelligence can revolutionize the way we engage with our congregations, optimize our resources, and deepen our spiritual journeys. As we move forward, let us embrace this technological advancement with open hearts and minds, leveraging its potential to enhance our ministries and spread the message of love, hope, and faith.

Encouragement for Pastors and Ministry Leaders to Embrace AI

In recent years, the emergence of artificial intelligence (AI) has revolutionized various industries, and its impact on the world is undeniable. As pastors and ministry leaders, it is crucial for us to recognize the potential benefits and opportunities that AI can bring to our ministries and embrace this technology to enhance our outreach efforts.

One of the key advantages of AI is its ability to analyze vast amounts of data and provide valuable insights. As pastors, we are constantly seeking ways to better understand and connect with our congregations. AI can help us make sense of the data we have, such as attendance records, sermon feedback, and engagement metrics, to gain deeper insights into the needs and preferences of our community. This knowledge can then be utilized to tailor our messages, programs, and outreach initiatives to better serve our congregants.

Furthermore, AI can assist pastors in delivering personalized pastoral care. By utilizing AI-powered chatbots or virtual assistants, we can provide round-the-clock support and guidance to those in need. These AI systems can offer prayer suggestions, and Bible verses, and even engage in meaningful conversations to offer comfort and encouragement to individuals facing various challenges.

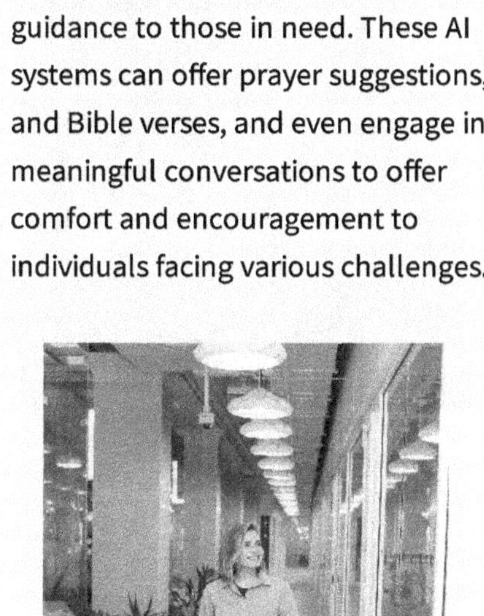

This personalized approach can help us extend our ministry's reach and impact, even beyond the physical limitations of our church walls.

Moreover, AI can be a valuable tool for sermon preparation. With the help of AI-powered algorithms, pastors can access a vast array of theological resources, sermons, and commentaries, allowing for a more comprehensive understanding of scripture and facilitating the creation of well-informed and impactful messages. AI can also assist in language translation, making it easier to connect with diverse communities and share the message of love and hope.

While some may be apprehensive about the integration of AI in ministry, it is important to remember that technology is not meant to replace human connection but rather enhance it. As pastors, our role remains essential in providing spiritual guidance, mentorship, and pastoral care that AI cannot replicate. Embracing AI will allow us to leverage its capabilities to further enhance our ministries, increase our effectiveness, and engage with our congregations in deeper and more meaningful ways.

Again, It is evident, AI has the potential to revolutionize the way pastors and ministry leaders carry out their work. By embracing AI, we can gain valuable insights, offer personalized pastoral care, and enhance sermon preparation, ultimately strengthening our ministries and expanding our outreach. Let us not fear this technology but instead embrace it as a powerful tool to advance the Kingdom of God and bring hope and transformation to our communities.

Final Thoughts on AI's Potential to Transform Ministry

As we conclude our exploration of artificial intelligence's potential to transform ministry, it is essential to reflect on the profound impact this technology can have on kingdom builders. The integration of AI into the realm of ministry brings with it a multitude of possibilities that can enhance and revolutionize the way we engage with our congregations and communities.

One of the most significant advantages AI offers to pastors is the ability to streamline administrative tasks, thus freeing up valuable time for more meaningful interactions with their congregations. By automating routine processes such as scheduling, data analysis, and communication, pastors can focus on cultivating deeper relationships, providing personalized spiritual guidance, and fostering a sense of community within their congregations.

Moreover, AI-powered tools can assist pastors in delivering more relevant and impactful sermons. By analyzing vast amounts of biblical texts, historical context, and contemporary issues, AI algorithms can generate valuable insights and help pastors craft sermons that resonate with their congregations' specific needs. This technology can also aid in sermon preparation, enabling pastors to research and reference relevant content more efficiently.

For business owners and professionals within the ministry, AI presents opportunities to improve operational efficiency and optimize decision-making processes. From managing finances to strategizing outreach initiatives, AI algorithms can provide valuable data-driven insights that empower leaders to make informed decisions, allocate resources effectively, and enhance overall organizational effectiveness.

Young people, who are often tech-savvy and accustomed to interacting with intelligent virtual assistants, can benefit from AI-driven educational tools designed to deepen their understanding of scripture and faith. AI-powered virtual mentors can engage young minds through interactive conversations, answering questions, and fostering a continuous learning environment.

Lastly, AI holds tremendous potential in the field of education, enabling teachers to provide personalized instruction tailored to students' individual needs. By leveraging AI's adaptive learning capabilities, educators can identify areas where students may be struggling, deliver targeted support, and offer a more customized learning experience.

While AI undoubtedly offers immense possibilities for transformation, it is crucial to approach its integration in ministry with thoughtful consideration and ethical discernment. As kingdom builders, it is essential to strike a balance between leveraging AI's capabilities and upholding the core values of compassion, empathy, and human connection.

In in nutshell, the potential of AI to transform ministry is vast. By embracing this technology, pastors can focus on building meaningful relationships, business owners can optimize organizational effectiveness, professionals can make informed decisions, young people can deepen their understanding, and teachers can provide personalized education. As we embark on this journey, let us remember to use AI as a tool to enhance our ministry, while never losing sight of the importance of human connection and the values that lie at the heart of our faith.

www.ingramcontent.com/pod-product-compliance
Lightning Source LLC
Chambersburg PA
CBHW071608270726
48661CB00019B/1647